Publisher's note
This early edition includes
two repeat illustrations,
since amended.

Travels with my sketchbook

Holidays, Work and Christmas

David Charsley

Travels with my sketchbook

David Charsley

ISBN 9781912821952

A CIP catalogue record for this book
is available from the British Library
Published 2021 Tricorn Books
131 High Street, Portsmouth,
PO1 2HW

Printed & bound in the UK

Travels with my sketchbook

A collection of sketches and visuals to either recapture experiences

or to stimulate discussion.

Using a variety of media including pencil,

felt tips to ink and watercolour.

These sketches began in 1966 whilst on holiday at Morthoe, Devon. The children were happily exploring rock pools, building sandcastles and paddling. I found the rock strata fascinating which prompted me to sketch with the only tool at hand, a Pantone felt tip.

Thereafter, I made a point of taking a pad, pencil or ink pen with me, so in time with the girls now more interested in markets and shops, left me to doodle to my heart's content.

Escuzels, France ‘81

Escuzels, France '81

Hele Bay, Devon

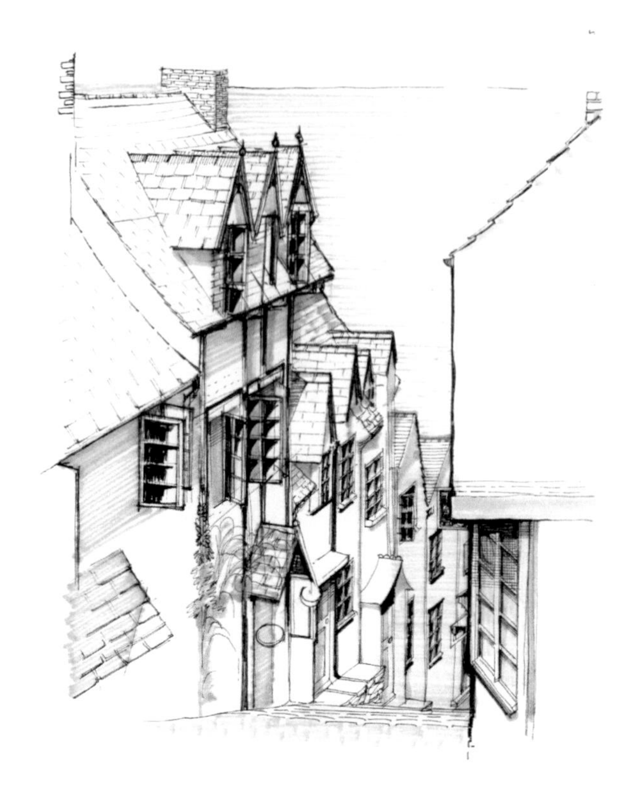

Clovelly, Devon '80

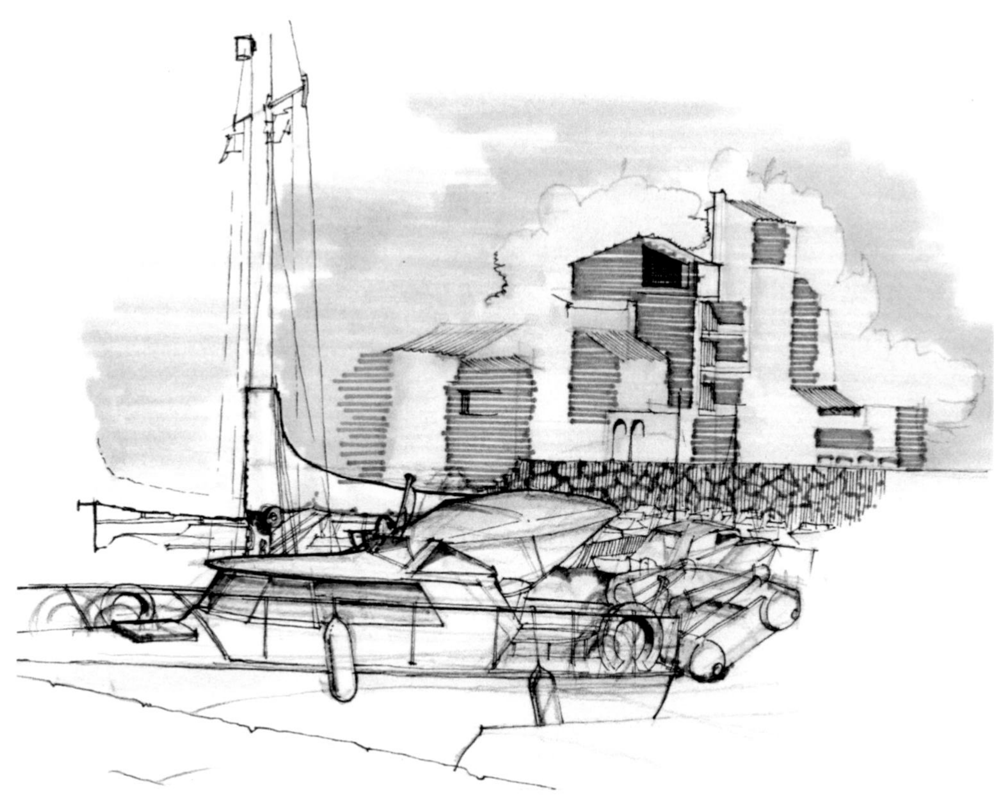

The Marina, Estartit. Spain '83

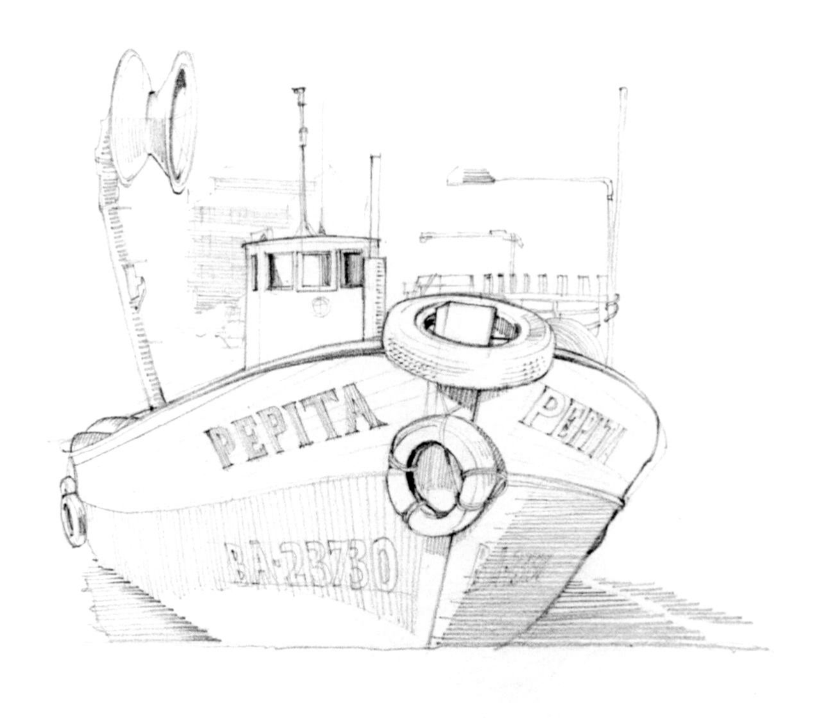

The Harbour, Estartit. Spain '83

The Harbour, Estartit. Spain '83

Tintagel, Cornwall '84

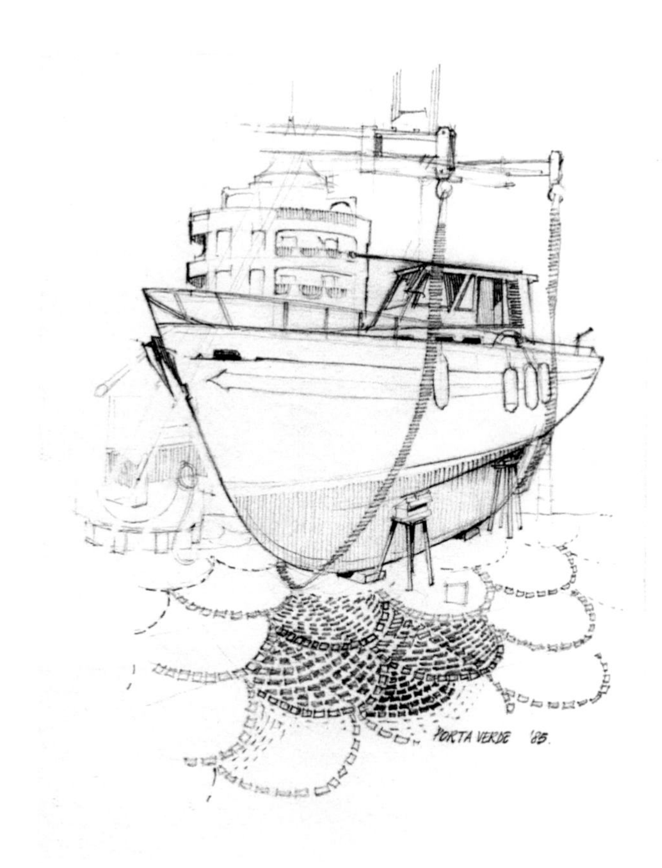

Porto Verde, Italy '85

Woolacombe

Ports Isaac, Cornwall

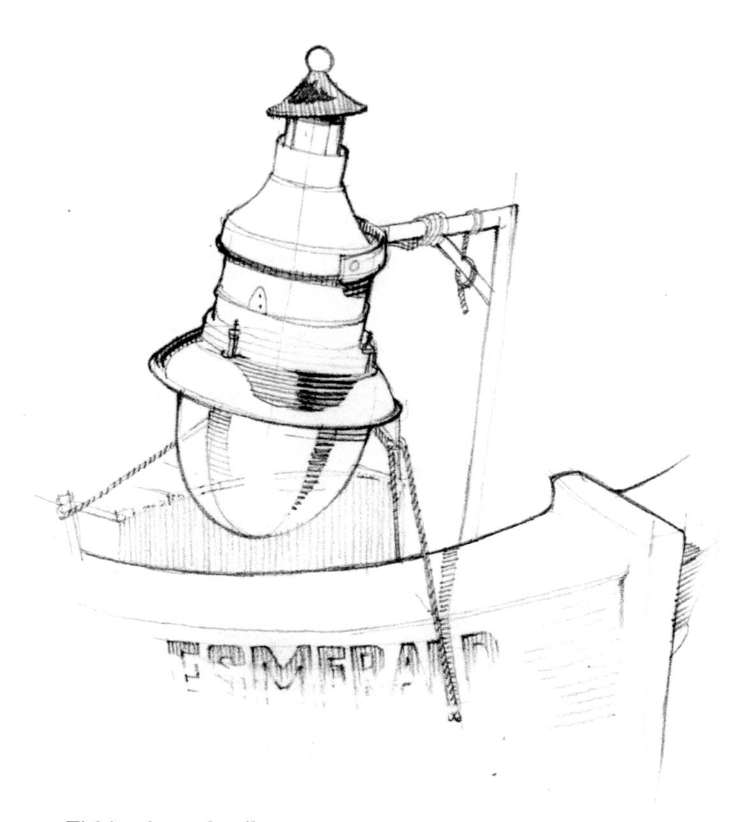

Fishing boat detail

Rotherwick Village Hall '15

St Ives harbour, Cornwall

Island Chapel, St Ives '08

Middlecombe Farm, Devon ‘08

Sherfield Oaks GC ‘04

La Greve Blanche, Brittany

Lake Maggiore

Middlecombe Farm, Devon '08

Plouguerneau, Brittany '08

Bere Regis, Dorset meadow '06

A friend had asked me to draw her cottage for a Christmas card, which prompted me to then produce my own of local subjects. That tradition has continued over the years.

Chesterwood House

Erdesley House '03

Royal Oak, Lasham

Golden Lion '14

Jane's Chawton 'pad'

St Mary's Overton

Longparish meadow '17

Alresford '12

In support of the dealer network overseas I acted as a link with BOTB*, Commerce and Trade organisations exhibitions, enabling products to be promoted in their respective region. Usually shell scheme stands, but invariably was able to persuade the organizers to provide open space, subject to approval. Some sketches were during 'down time' when there was a lull in activity or views from hotel rooms.

*British Overseas Trade Board

Trondheim. Norway '74

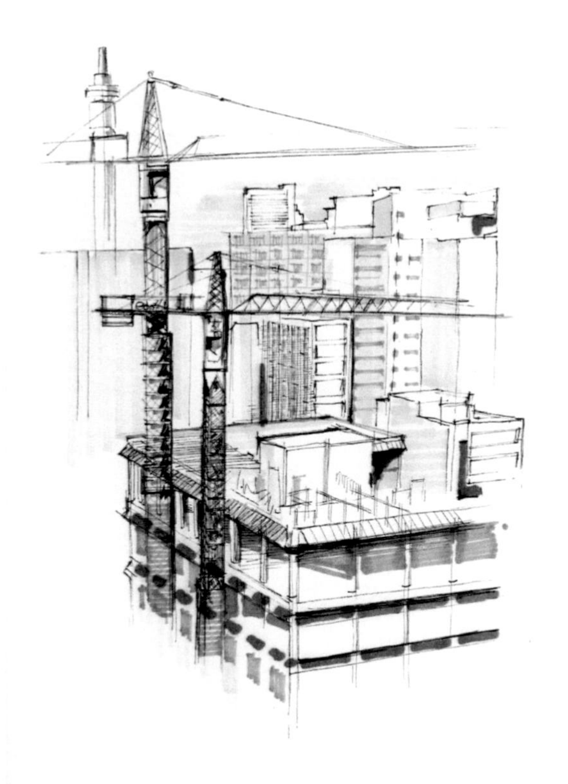

Jo'burg SA '74

Changi, Singapore '79

Trans '76 . Holland

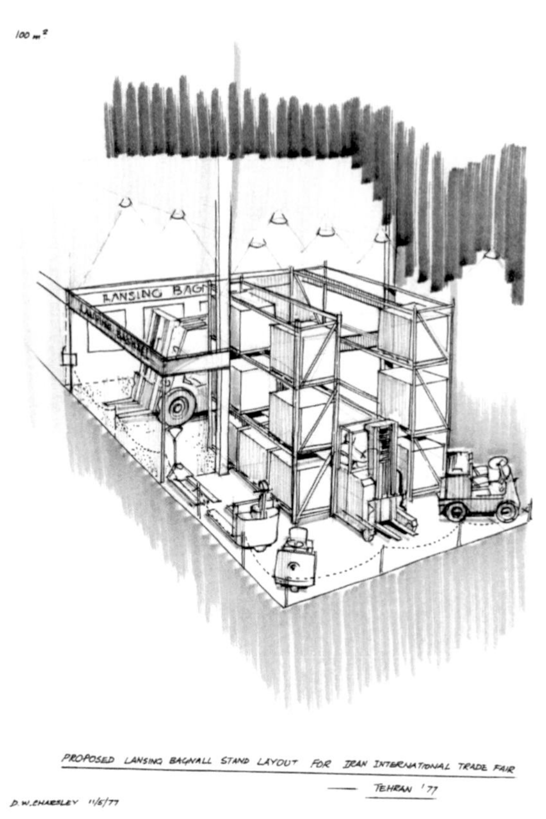

Tehran Trade Fair, Iran '77

Sydney Harbour '79

Wellington Trade Fair, NZ '75

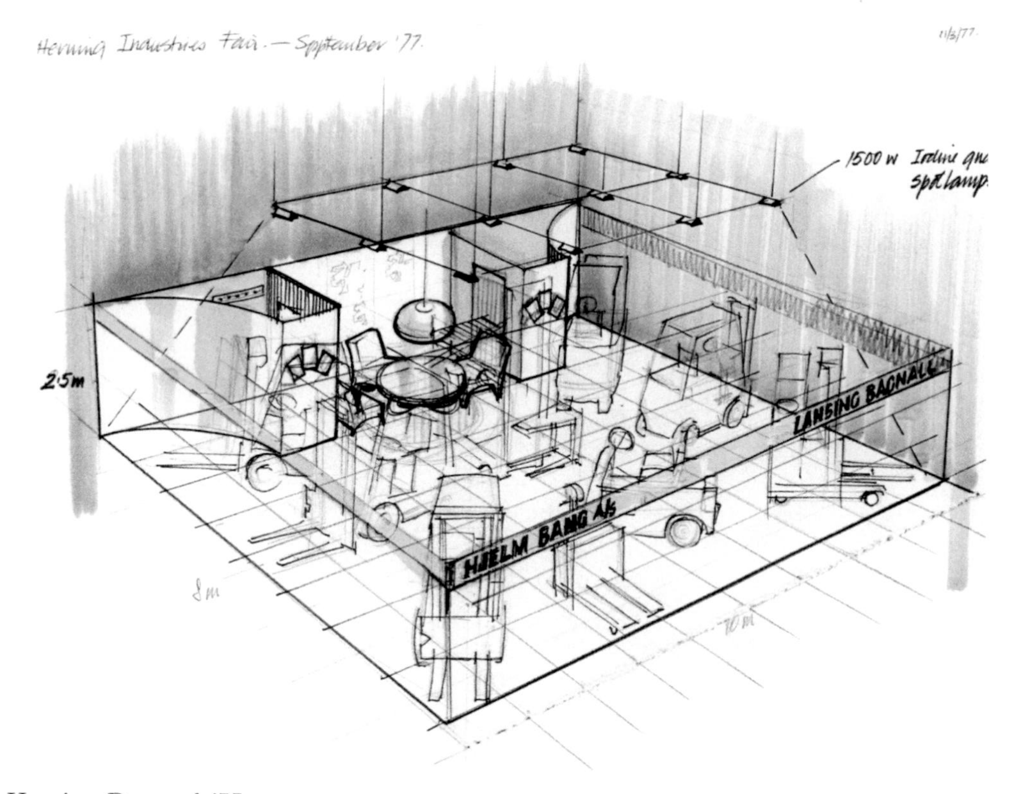

Herning, Denmark '77

Arlanda Airport, Sweden '76

A collection of ‘odds and ends’ that don’t fit into any of the categories … just a ‘bin’.

LIONS CLUB OF BASINGSTOKE
Present the 2nd
PRO-AM
TOURNAMENT

BY KIND PERMISSION OF THE DIRECTORS
AND MEMBERS
BASINGSTOKE GOLF CLUB
SUNDAY 29TH JULY
IN AID OF A TYMPANOMETER FOR BASINGSTOKE DISTRICT HOSPITAL
FURTHER DETAILS INCLUDING SPONSORSHIP FROM :
ALEX WALLACE
LONG SUTTON 81776
OR
BERNARD HARRINGTON
BASINGSTOKE 65394

Golf poster

Rotherwick Village Hall '15

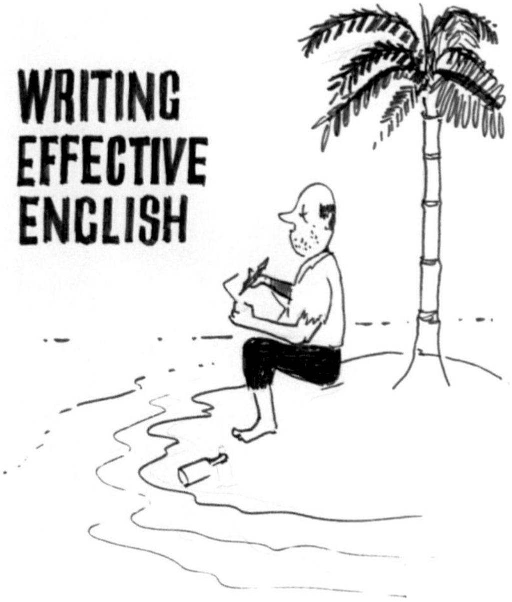

A visual for a book cover

The Carnival float

Giggle Golf
ENTRANCE INCLUDING REFRESHMENTS
50p
TICKETS AT THE BAR
10 holes stableford
on (½ handicap)
Thursday 22ND July
TWO CLUBS & A PUTTER * STARTING TIMES FROM 5·30p.m. * LIST ON MAIN BOARD

Golf poster

'In days of yore
Knights went to war
Seen astride their chargers.
Latterday Knights now stack at heights
On trucks with built-in chargers!'

E Kaye's Knighthood. '74

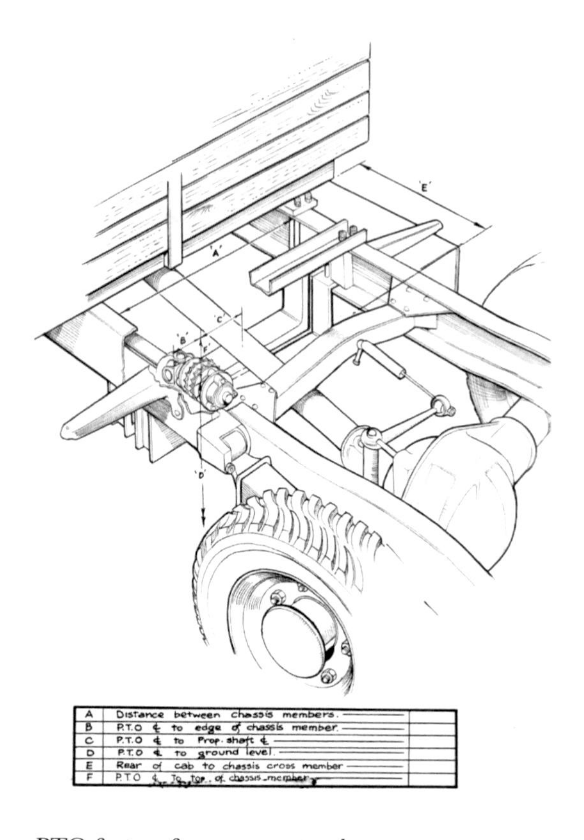

PTO feature for recovery truck

Dorset steam rally

BASINGSTOKE GOLF CLUB

ANNUAL DINNER & DANCE

ON FRIDAY 11TH FEBRUARY

7-30 for 8·00

AT

HAMPSHIRE HOUSE HOTEL

NAMES ON LIST PLEASE - MONIES PAYABLE, AT THE BAR BY 4/2/77.

Golf poster

Preston Candover

Lymington Quay '09

L'Estartit '83

Cliddesden Lynchgate '06

Cliddesden school '86

Erdesley House '03

Basingstoke Golf Club '16

Runnymeade Hotel '11

Northington Church '17

Adrian's gone to bed

Plumineux, France

Lymington Quay '09

Mousehole

Travels with my sketchbook